ST. FRANCIS
AT
PRAYER

W. Bader

ST. FRANCIS AT PRAYER

New City Press

First published in English language in Great Britain by
Darton, Longman and Todd Ltd., London
©1988 Darton, Longman and Todd Ltd.

Published in the United States by New City Press
206 Skillman Avenue, Brooklyn, New York 11211

Translated from the original German edition
Franz von Assisi — Gebete by Alan Neame
©1986 Verlag Neue Stadt GmbH, Munich 83, Germany

Cover design by Nick Cianfarani

Library of Congress Cataloging-in-Publication Data:

Francis, of Assisi, Saint, 1182-1226.
   [Prayers.   English. Selections]
   St. Francis at Prayer / W. Bader, ed.
     p. cm.
   Translation of: Gebete.
   ISBN 0-911782-80-X : $6.95
   1. Prayers, Medieval.   I. Bader, Wolfgang, 1948- II. Title.
  III. Title: Saint Francis at prayer.
BV245.F673 1990
242'.802 — dc20

                                           90-3997

Printed in the United States of America

Table of Contents

Translator's Note

In compiling his Office of the Passion, St. Francis used the Latin psalms (Vlg.). His occasional prayers and hymns, with the notable exception of *The Canticle of the Creatures,* have also been transmitted in Latin and, like the Office psalms, exist in a number of variant forms.

A major source for the anecdotal material is Friar Thomas of Celano who joined the Franciscan movement in about 1214 and wrote two biographies of the saint, the first (1 Cel) completed in 1229 three years after the latter's death, the second (2 Cel) in 1247.

Where appropriate, scriptural quotations are from *The New Jerusalem Bible.*

Alan Neame

Introduction

Properly speaking, our personal relationship with God admits of no third-party observer. Nowhere are we more defenseless than when standing in the presence of our Creator. There we are truly ourselves; there we neither need nor can misrepresent the facts or make excuses, since our Creator knows us better than we know ourselves.

Francis was not one of those Christians who composed a treatise on the spiritual life. Nor did he chronicle the stages as he followed in the footsteps of Jesus. In this respect, no doubt, he was a true servant of his Lady Poverty in that he shrank from reporting God's favors, to avoid the acclamation and admiration of others. The Poverello commends as blessed that "servant who lays up the graces the Lord has bestowed on him, as treasure in heaven; who keeps the Lord's secrets and has no desire to publish them for the sake of human approval; for God in his own good time will make his works known."[1] Hence, to find out about Francis' inner life, we have to study his (few) writings and the (many) notes and accounts of his life originating from soon after his death.

The outset of his spiritual journey was marked by deep shock at experiencing God's love. Francis was still living in his father's house. One night, when revelling

1. *Admonitions 28.*

through Assisi with some of his drinking companions, his heart was suddenly filled with such bliss that he lost all other sensation. So completely did this bliss seize on all his physical senses that — as he himself was later to relate — he could not have moved, had he been cut to pieces on the spot . . . from that hour on, he determined to harbor Jesus Christ in his heart. Often, indeed daily, he felt the need to commune in secret with his heavenly Father. A bliss, suddenly overwhelming him, constrained him to this. From the street or wherever he happened to be, it drew him away to pray.[1]

The experience of God's favor compelled him to respond: " 'The love that has loved us so much, we must love as much in return' . . . He could never hear the words *God's love* without undergoing a kind of transformation; for immediately on hearing these words he was aroused, stirred, inflamed as though some inner chord of his heart were being touched by the plectrum of an outward voice."[2]

Francis experienced God's presence in his heart. He became ever more clearly aware that the Triune God, Father, Son and Holy Spirit, had taken up residence in him — and that everyone who followed him would experience the same. Hence in his *Unconfirmed Rule* he writes: "Within our hearts we must prepare a home and dwelling place for God our Lord, the almighty Father, the Son and the Holy Spirit.[3]

His intimate friendship with God expressed itself in a variety of ways: sometimes he would address Him respectfully as though his feudal lord, sometimes he would answer as to a judge, sometimes he would entreat

1. *Cf. Legend of the Three Companions 7-8.*
2. *2 Cel 196.*
3. *Unconfirmed Rule 22.*

9

Him as though a father, sometimes converse with Him as with a friend and make merry with him as with a bridegroom.[1]

"His safest haven was prayer," wrote Thomas of Celano, the earliest of the saint's biographers, "and this did not last for a mere moment but for as long as possible. If he began late, he scarce ended by morning. Walking, sitting, eating or drinking, he was ever intent on prayer."[2] "The brothers moreover who lived with him knew how constantly every day his talk was of Jesus, how sweet and tender was his discourse, how benign and full of love his conversation. Out of the abundance of the heart his mouth spoke. Ever did he bear Jesus in his heart, Jesus in his mouth, Jesus in his ears, Jesus in his eyes, Jesus in his hands, Jesus in his other members. Oh, how often, when sitting at table, if he heard or named or thought of Jesus, would he forget the bodily food!"[3]

In this intimate union with Jesus, Thomas of Celano also sees the reason for Francis later receiving the stigmata on Mount Alverna: "Because with wondrous love he ever bore and preserved in his heart Christ Jesus and Him crucified, therefore was he signed above all other men with His sign."[4]

Seeking guidance from the Gospel

For Francis of Assisi who had received no theological training, a loving heart was his key to Holy Scripture: "He would occasionally read the sacred books; and

1. *Cf. 2 Cel 95.*
2. *1 Cel 71.*
3. *1 Cel 115.*
4. *Ibid.*

what he had once put into his mind, he wrote indelibly on his heart. Memory supplied the place of books; if he heard a thing once, it was not in vain, because his affection ruminated it with continual devotion. This, he said, was the fruitful way to read, not by picking one's way through a thousand treatises."[1]

For him the words of Holy Writ, which he also called the "words of the Holy Spirit," were a source from which he drew light and strength. To Bernard of Quintavalle, the first brother to join him, he once announced, "Let us go to church early in the morning, consult the book of gospels and seek Christ's advice!"[2] Francis who, as Thomas of Celano remarks, did not listen to the Gospel as one deaf, took good care "to fulfil the word of God diligently to the letter."[3] In it he recognized the will of God for him: "No one showed me the way; it was the Lord himself who revealed to me that I was to live according to the Holy Gospel."[4] This rule of life was to apply to all the members of the Franciscan Order for all time. The Rule of their Order begins with the words: To observe the Gospel of our Lord Jesus Christ through a life of obedience, without possessions and in chastity. This was no dead letter. A contemporary chronicle bears witness: "The Friars Minor dwelled in the town and lived by the Gospel."

---

1. *2 Cel 102.*
2. *2 Cel 15.*
3. *1 Cel 22.*
4. *Testament, 14.*

The Eucharist: God's humility

The love Francis bore Jesus in the Sacrament of the Altar is one of the unfathomable secrets of his life. "He communicated often and so devoutly that others too began to honor Christ devoutly in his Eucharistic form."[1]

To all his brothers he wrote (1224): "I beseech you, Brothers, kissing your feet, and with all the love of which I am able, to pay all devotion and honor to the most holy Body and Blood of our Lord Jesus Christ."

He admonished his brothers with the words: "Daily the Son of God demeans himself, as he did long ago when he left his kingly throne to enter the Virgin's womb. Daily he comes to us in person. Daily he descends from the Father's bosom on to the altar. And as he showed himself in human form to the Apostles, so now he shows himself to us in the sacred Host. And as the former only saw his flesh and yet believed that he was God, so we too, who see the bread and wine, must firmly believe that his is his true and living Body and Blood."[2]

The sacrament of the creation

The rich merchant's son who one day renounced his home with the words "No more *Father Bernardone* but *Our Father in heaven* . . ." found many brothers and sisters along life's path. The first Chapter General, summoned by Francis in 1219, was attended by more than 5,000 brothers. But he became a brother not only to other human beings but to the creatures as well, for

1. *Bonaventure, Life of St. Francis IX, 2.*
2. *Admonitions 1.*

they had the same Creator and Father. "In fair things he beheld Him who is most fair and, through the traces of Himself which He has left imprinted on His creatures, he everywhere followed on to reach the Beloved."[1]

The poet of *The Canticle of the Creatures,* the preacher to whom the birds paid heed, the saint who struck a peace treaty with a wolf, was also concerned that the bees should get food in winter and not have to suffer from the cold.[2] "For their part, the creatures did all they could to show him their gratitude. They rejoiced in his caresses, granted his requests and obeyed his commands."[3]

When, on 30 September 1224, Francis bade farewell to Mount Alverna, he not only saluted his brothers but said, "Farewell, Mount Alverna! Farewell, dear Brother Falcon! Thank you for the love you have shown me. Farewell, lofty peak! I shall never be able to visit you again. Farewell, rock that enfolded me in your vault, thus playing a trick on the Evil One. We shall never see one another again . . ."[4]

Reverence for all people

When Francis was writing his testament, he looked back on that first encounter in which he grasped what Jesus meant by saying, "In so far as you did this to the least of my brothers, you did it to me" (Mt 25:40). He wrote: "When I was still living in my sins, I found the

1. *Bonaventure, Life of St. Francis IX, 1.*
2. *Cf. 1 Cel 80.*
3. *2 Cel 166.*
4. *Little Flowers of St. Francis 57a.*

sight of lepers revolting. But the Lord himself led me to them. I served them and in the course of time I noticed that what had seemed bitter to me was transformed into sweetness of spirit and body."[1]

In serving others, he served the Lord himself;[2] in the poor he recognized the face of the suffering Christ. Whenever anything was given to him, he gave it away as an absolute matter of course, since he was convinced it was incumbent on everyone to help the poor. On the way to Siena he explained to a brother why he had given his cloak away in spite of the cold: "We must return this cloak to the poor man to whom it belongs. It was only on loan to us until we came across someone poorer than ourselves."[3] He taught another brother: "Whenever you see a poor man, a mirror of the Lord and his poor mother is set before you."[4]

His love of the cross

Christ crucified stands at the beginning and the end of his spiritual journey. At San Damiano, Francis heard the voice from the crucifix summoning him to repair the ruinous house of the Lord. On Mount Alverna, by a special grace, he became like Christ in receiving the marks of the wounds of the crucified Lord.

So truly was Francis orientated towards the good thing that God had in store for him that he bade every

1. *Testament 1-3.*
2. *1 Cel 17.*
3. *2 Cel 87.*
4. *2 Cel 85.*

kind of suffering welcome[1] or, as Thomas of Celano puts it, "He chose the bitter in preference to the sweet."[2] As witness his definition of perfect joy which he dictated to his secretary Brother Leo:

Suppose we received the news that all the learned men of Paris had entered the Order . . . Write: "This is not true joy." Or again, all the prelates and bishops beyond the Alps and the King of France and the King of England to boot . . . Write: "This is not true joy." Suppose our brothers had converted all the infidels and I possessed the gift of healing the sick and of working all sorts of miracles . . . I tell you: Even this is not true joy.

But suppose I come home one icy night from Perugia; icicles have formed round the bottom of my tunic and, banging against my shins, have made them bleed. Frozen and filthy, I arrive at the door. I knock and call until a brother comes. And when I say to him, "I am Brother Francis," he refuses to let me in, saying, "Go away, you stupid dolt. We don't need the likes of you here." Even after much pleading he will not be prevailed on to admit me even for a single night . . . If I am patient through all this, Fra Leo, that is true joy . . . [3]

Francis, how ought we to pray?

God in his heart, in Holy Scripture, in bread and wine,

1. *First Consideration on the Sacred Stigmata.*
2. *2 Cel 9.*
3. *Opuscula p. 461; cf. Little Flowers 8.*

in his neighbor, in the creation and in suffering: all these sources enrich Francis in his confident relationship with him whom he loves above all. One might now demonstrate the various strands of his prayer-life, investigating the liturgical and biblical sources and references, but in so doing one would certainly destroy something that was an indivisible whole. Prayer, love and action in everyday life were differing but complementary aspects of the life of the saint, of whom it was said that he of all people most resembled Christ. "He was not merely a man who prayed; his whole existence had become a prayer."[1]

If we could ask him, as his companions did:[2] "Francis, how should we pray?" he would certainly give us the same answer as he gave them: "When you pray, say *Our Father* . . ." And this is where Francis' prayer-life yields up its secret: of being simple like Jesus. Don't we all yearn for this sort of simplicity? And who could be a better brother to us on this path than Francis?

Wolfgang Bader

1. *2 Cel 95.*
2. *1 Cel 45.*

16

On the Path of Life

"Through his life,
spring burst upon the world."
(Legend of the Three Companions)

Before the crucifix in San Damiano

Francis, the son of a well-to-do cloth merchant, was already twenty-five years old when, in the church of San Damiano, he received the call to repair the ruined house of God. Before the famous crucifix, now preserved in the church of St. Clare at Assisi, he answered the Lord in the following prayer (being the earliest one of his recorded):

Most high and glorious God,
lighten the darkness of my heart
and give me sound faith,
firm hope
and perfect love.
Let me, Lord, have the right feelings
and knowledge,
properly to carry out
the task you have given me.

(2 Cel 10)

In response to God's love

May the burning and tender might
of your love,
I beseech you, O Lord,
ravish my soul
from all earthly things:
so that I may die
for love of my love.

Recorded by the Franciscan friar Ubertino da Casale
(1273-1317) in his work *Arbor Vitae Crucifixae Jesu*
V/4. Although not composed by Francis himself, it was
a prayer he loved to use.

Poverty: my only riches

Lord, show me Poverty
whom you loved so dearly.
Merciful Jesus,
have pity on me:
I am full of yearning
for my Lady Poverty;
I can find no peace without her.
You, Lord, it was who first
aroused love for her in my heart;
grant me the privilege
of possessing her.
I yearn to be enriched
by this treasure.
I earnestly implore you,
it may belong to me and mine forever.
Jesus, you were very poor,
and I want to call
nothing under heaven mine
but only to live
on what others may give me.

Recorded by Ubertino da Casale in *Arbor Vitae* 19-21.

Everything I have is yours

My Lord,
I am all yours.
You know
I have nothing
besides my tunic, cord and underpants.
And even these three things are yours.
So what can I give you?

(Third Consideration on the Sacred Stigmata)

Like the tax collector in the temple

To pray, Francis liked to withdraw to some lonely place. Once when he was "waiting in fear and trembling upon the ruler of the whole world and thinking in the bitterness of his soul about his past years ill-spent, he kept repeating the words (of the tax collector in St. Luke's Gospel, 18:13) over and over again:

God,
be merciful to me, a sinner!

Then unspeakable joy began to fill his heart and the certainty was granted him that all his sins were forgiven!"

(1 Cel 26)

My all

Once, when Francis thought his companion, Brother Bernard, was asleep, he got up when all was quiet, raised his eyes and arms to heaven and throughout the night until morning kept repeating the words:

My God,
my God . . .

The Little Flowers explains that, in this prayer drawn from the heart, Francis was contemplating the greatness of God; that he had understood the divine plan for his Order and become aware of his personal inadequacy.

(Little Flowers 1)

God's treasures

Francis enjoyed contemplation of God in a uniquely immediate way. These encounters completely transformed him. However, on returning from his private prayers to human society, he was at great pains that no one should observe anything of these intimate meetings with the Lord. Francis advised his brothers in similar situations to say this prayer:

Lord, I am an unworthy
and sinful man;
the consolation
you have sent me from heaven
I return into your hands;
if not, I should feel like a thief
appropriating your treasure for myself.

(Bonaventure, Life of St. Francis X, 4)

Confession of guilt

I confess all my sins
to the Lord, God the Father,
the Son and the Holy Spirit,
to Blessed Mary ever virgin,
to all the saints in heaven and on earth,
to Brother Elias
Minister General of our Order
my venerable Superior,
to the priests
and all brothers of our Order:
in many ways I have offended
through my grievous fault,
particularly in not having kept the Rule
which I promised to the Lord;
and in not having said the Office
as the Rule commands,
whether from negligence,
or owing to ill-health,
or because I am an ignorant
and uneducated man.

From a letter Francis wrote to the Chapter General
and all the friars in about 1220.

We adore you

Of the following prayer, Thomas of Celano writes: "On one occasion the brothers entreated Francis to teach them how to pray, for as yet they did not know how to say the offices of the Church. The saint replied: 'When you pray, say *Our Father...* and *We adore you*'

"Whenever they passed a church, they bowed down to show their reverence with body and soul, even if it could only be seen in the distance. They prayed as Francis had taught them. And whenever they caught sight of a cross or the mark of a cross along their way, whether on the trees or hedges, they did the same."

Taken from the liturgy for the Feast of the Exaltation of the Cross (14 September), the prayer occurs in Francis' testament, dictated by him on the last day of his life (September/October 1226).

We adore you,
Lord Jesus Christ,
in all the churches
of the whole world
and we bless you,
for by means of your holy cross
you have redeemed the world.

(1 Cel 45; Legend of the Three Companions 37)

Greatness of the "Little Ones"

Astonished and disappointed at the hostile way distinguished and respected people reacted to his embassy of poverty, Francis spoke thus to the Lord:

Blessed are you,
Lord God,
for hiding these things
from the learned and clever
and revealing them to little children.
Yes, Father, for that is what it has pleased
you to do.
Jesus, Father and Lord of my life,
deliver me from their evil counsels
and suffer me not to fall
into similar condemnation,
but grant me by your grace
to find what I am seeking,
for I am your servant
and the son of your handmaid.

(The Holy Converse of the Blessed Francis with the Lady Poverty 2)

For his Brothers

Having learnt that two of his brothers had set a bad example, Francis weeping prayed to the Lord:

Lord Jesus Christ,
who chose the twelve Apostles,
and though one of them was lost,
the rest remained true to you
and preached the Gospel,
being filled with the Holy Spirit:
now, Lord, in your mercy
you have endowed the brothers with faith
so that they can strengthen others
and so fulfill the mystery of the Gospel.
Who then can make satisfaction
when the very ones whom you have sent
do not bear witness to the light
but instead do the works of darkness?

(2 Cel 156)

For the Order

At the Chapter General of the Order at Whitsun 1220, Francis resigned further responsibility for ruling the Order: "Henceforth I am dead to you. But here is Brother Peter Cattani whom we all, you and I, will obey." Whereupon he bowed down before him and promised him obedience and reverence. The brothers then began to weep; great was their grief on seeing themselves as it were abandoned as orphans. Francis clasped his hands and raising his eyes to heaven said:

To you, Lord, I commend this family
which you committed to my care until today.
By reason of my infirmity, which you know,
my sweetest Lord,
I can no longer sustain the care of it.
I commend it also to the Provincial Ministers;
they will answer for it
at the day of judgement
if any brother, by their negligence
or by their bad example
or their too harsh correction,
should perish.

(2 Cel 143)

The power of humility

In the summer of 1224 Francis took Brothers Leo, Masseo and Angelo with him to Mount Alverna. On the way they took refuge in a deserted church on account of a storm. While the three brothers slept, Francis was tormented by evil spirits. Then he cried with a loud voice:

My Lord Jesus Christ,
I thank you
for the great love and charity
you show me.
For it is a sign of great love
when the Lord punishes his servant
for all his misdeeds in this world
rather than punish him in the next.
And I am joyfully prepared
to undergo every trial
and every adversity which you, God,
are pleased to send me
for my sins.

The Little Flowers observes: "Then the demons, confused and vanquished by his constancy and patience, departed."

(Little Flowers 55)

31

A Father's worries

One day Francis was thinking about his death and the future of the Order. When he uttered the following prayer, an angel of the Lord appeared and comforted him, saying there was no need for him to be worried, for the Order would never fail till the day of judgement.

Lord my God
after my death what will become
of this your poor little family
which, of your goodness,
you have entrusted to me, a sinner?
Who will comfort them?
Who will correct them?
Who will pray to you for them?

(2nd Consideration on the Sacred Stigmata)

"I am a worm . . ." (Ps 22:7)

One night, before the Feast of the Exaltation of the Cross in the year 1224, Brother Leo overheard Francis endlessly repeating the following words:

Who are you,
O my most sweet God,
and who am I,
most vile worm
and your worthless servant?

When the astonished brother asked for an explanation, the saint replied: "I was shown two lights and realized who the Creator is and who I am. I saw the depths of the infinite goodness of God and the deplorable depths of my own nothingness. That is why I said:

Who are you,
Lord of infinite goodness,
wisdom and power,
who deign to visit me,
a vile and abominable worm?"

(3rd Consideration on the Sacred Stigmata)

Loving and suffering like Jesus

The day before Francis was imprinted with the marks of Christ's passion, he turned towards the sun and prayed:

My Lord Jesus Christ,
two graces I beg of you
before I die:
the first is that in my lifetime
I may feel, in my soul and in my body,
as far as possible,
that sorrow which you, sweet Jesus,
endured in the hour
of your most bitter passion;
the second is that I may feel in my heart,
as far as possible,
that abundance of love with which you,
Son of God,
were inflamed, so as willingly to endure
so great a passion for us sinners.

(3rd Consideration on the Sacred Stigmata)

The Divine Praises

When Francis was staying on Mount Alverna after receiving the marks of Christ's passion (1224, two years before his death), Brother Leo desired to have something written in the saint's own hand. He hoped by means of it to be freed from a grievous spiritual temptation, but he was shy of bothering Francis on the subject. The latter however summoned him and said, "Bring me parchment and ink." The brother instantly obeyed and Francis with his own hand wrote the following Divine Praises and a blessing for Brother Leo (cf. 2 Cel 49).

You are holy, Lord,
the only God,
and your deeds are wonderful.
You are strong,
you are great,
you are the Most High,
you are the almighty King.
You, holy Father,
are King of heaven and earth.
You are three and one,
God above all gods.
You are good, all good, supreme good,
Lord God, living and true.
You are love,

you are wisdom,
you are humility,
you are endurance,
you are beauty,
you are gentleness,
you are security,
you are rest,
you are joy.
You are our hope and happiness,
you are justice and moderation,
you are all our riches,
you are beauty,
you are gentleness,
you are our protector,
you are our guardian and defender.
You are strength,
you are consolation,
you are our hope,
you are our faith,
you are our love,
you are all our sweetness,
you are our eternal life,
great and admirable Lord,
God almighty,
merciful Savior.

A blessing for Brother Leo

May the Lord bless you and keep you,
may he show his face to you
and have mercy on you,
may he turn to you and give you peace,
may the Lord bless you, Brother Leo.

On this sheet of parchment, which Brother Leo always carried on his person, he noted: "The Blessed Francis wrote this blessing with his own hand for me, Brother Leo." The phrasing is borrowed almost word for word from the blessing Aaron was enjoined to pronounce over the Israelites (cf. 6:24-6).

Lord, help me

Francis suffered ever more severely from a disease of the eyes; henceforward he found not only daylight unbearable but firelight too. For further treatment he made a journey to Rieti in 1225, stopping for a while on the way in a cell at San Damiano in Assisi. There he was annoyed by countless mice, allowing him no peace by day or night. In this condition, he turned to God:

> Lord Jesus Christ,
> you are the good shepherd.
> You grant us
> your loving mercy
> without our having deserved it,
> and many a time it must endure
> the pangs of sharp pain.
> Since you have called me to your flock,
> I beg you by your grace and strength
> that in trouble, anguish and distress
> I may never turn away from you.

Then he loudly called:

> Lord,
> look down on me in my infirmities
> and help me to bear them patiently.

Thomas of Celano relates how Francis, while in prayer, received the word of the Lord: "Rejoice, for your sickness is the earnest of my kingdom. Since you have been so patient, you can with certainty await this kingdom." To which Francis replied:

I will rejoice
at my tribulations and infirmities
and be strong in the Lord,
at all times giving thanks to God the Father
and to his only Son
our Lord Jesus Christ
and to the Holy Spirit,
for the great grace he has given me
in deigning to assure me,
his unworthy servant,
while I am still alive,
that his kingdom will be mine.

(Mirror of Perfection C)

The Canticle of the Creatures

The Canticle of the Creatures is without question the most famous of St. Francis' prayers. It is closely bound up with his life. The first strophe was composed by the saint when, gravely ill and inwardly depressed, he was staying by the church of San Damiano (1224/1225). An authentic composition by Francis, the *Canticle* was written in Old Italian and is one of the most important literary witnesses to the popular language of the period.

"As long ago the three children in the burning fiery furnace invited all the elements to praise and glorify the Creator, so in all his creatures Francis glorified the Creator and Governor of all things." Such is Thomas of Celano's comment on *The Canticle of the Creatures.*[1]

Bonaventure, the most learned member of the Franciscan Order, who died in 1274, explained Francis' relationship to the creatures by a simile: "For by the impulse of his unexampled devotion he tasted that fountain of goodness that streams forth, as in rivulets, in every created thing, and he perceived as it were a heavenly harmony in the concord of properties and actions granted to them by God, and sweetly exhorted them to praise the Lord."[2]

When a quarrel broke out between the mayor and

---

1. *1 Cel 80.*
2. *Life of St. Francis IX, 1.*

40

bishop of Assisi, Francis added the strophe on forgiveness. Legend has it that they became reconciled when the brothers sang the canticle to them.

The strophe on Sister Death was composed when Francis felt himself approaching new life in 1226.

When his illness became very severe, he began singing the Canticle of the Creatures. And afterwards he had his brothers sing it so that in considering the praises of the Lord he might forget the bitterness of his pains and infirmities . . . He was wont to say: "In the morning when the sun rises, everyone ought to praise God who created it for our use, because thanks to it our eyes are enlightened by day. Then in the evening, when it gets dark, everyone ought to give praise on account of Brother Fire, thanks to whom our eyes are enlightened by night. And therefore we ought especially to praise the Creator himself for this and the other creatures which we daily use."[1]

Mirror of Perfection CXIX.

Most high, all-powerful, good Lord,
all praise be yours, all glory, all honor
and all blessing.
To you alone, Most High, do they belong.
No mortal lips are worthy
to pronounce your name.

All praise be yours, my Lord,
in all your creatures,
especially Sir Brother Sun
who brings the day;
and light you give us through him.
How beautiful he is, how radiant in his
splendor!
Of you, Most High, he is the token.

All praise be yours, my Lord
for Sister Moon and the Stars;
in the heavens you have made them,
bright and precious and fair.

All praise be yours, my Lord,
for Brother Wind and the Air,
and fair and stormy
and every kind of weather
by which you nourish everything
you have made.

All praise be yours, my Lord,
for Sister Water;
she is so useful and lowly,
so precious and pure.

All praise be yours, my Lord,
for Brother Fire
by whom you brighten the night.
How beautiful he is,
how gay, robust and strong!

All praise be yours, my Lord,
for Sister Earth, our mother
who feeds us, rules us
and produces all sorts of fruit
and colored flowers and herbs.

All praise be yours, my Lord,
for those who forgive one another
for love of you
and endure infirmity and tribulation.
Happy are they who endure these in peace
for by you, Most High, they will be crowned.

All praise be yours, my Lord,
for our Sister Physical Death
from whose embrace no mortal can escape.
Woe to those who die in mortal sin!
Happy are those she finds
doing your most holy will!
The second death can do no harm to them.

Praise and bless my Lord
and give him thanks and serve him
with great humility.

Dear Brother Fire

One day Francis' eye disease had to be treated by a surgeon with the cautery. To the fire heating the cauterizing iron, he said:

My Brother Fire,
outdoing all created things in splendor,
the Most High created you
mighty, fair and useful.
Be kind to me at this hour,
be courteous,
for I have long loved you in the Lord.
I pray the great Lord
who created you
to temper your heat now
so that, burning me gently,
I may be able to bear it.

(2 Cel 166)

When his illness got worse . . .

I thank you, Lord God,
for all my pains;
if it pleases you, Lord
increase them a hundredfold.
I shall thankfully accept
whatever sorrow you give,
not sparing me;
for in the fulfillment of your will
I find my greatest solace.

(Bonaventure, Life of St. Francis 14, 2)

A prayer for Assisi

When Francis felt his death was approaching, he had himself carried on a litter to the church of St. Mary of the Angels, wishing to die there where his new life had begun. On the way he asked the bearers to make a short halt and, having himself turned towards the town of Assisi, which on account of his blindness he could no longer descry, he uttered the following prayer:

Lord,
as in days gone by
many evil-doers lived in this city,
so now I see
it has pleased your abundant mercy
to show this city
the fullness of your grace.
May it become a dwelling and a home
for all who acknowledge you
and seek to glorify your name
forever and ever;
for all who give
an example of virtuous life
and witness of true doctrine
to all Christendom.
I therefore beg you,

Lord Jesus Christ,
Father of mercies,
not to consider our ingratitude
but ever to be mindful
of your abundant mercy
which you have displayed here.

(Mirror of Perfection 124)

His death

When Francis realized that the hour of his death had arrived, he called two of the brothers of whom he was particularly fond and charged them loudly to sing *The Canticle of the Creatures*. He himself, as well as he could, prayed Psalm 142:

> Loudly I cry to the Lord,
> listen to my entreaty . . .

He then said to Brother Elias: "God is calling me. I remit all the offenses and faults of my brothers absent as well as present. Make this known to them and bless them all for me.

> God the King of all
> bless you in heaven and on earth.
> I bless you as I can
> and more than I can.
> And what I cannot,
> may he who can do all things
> do in you.
> May you find every blessing you desire
> and may whatever you worthily ask
> come to pass for you."

To the doctor who was in attendance, he said: "Brother Physician, boldly tell me when death is actually at hand; it will be the gate to life for me."

With a blithe heart he bade death approach as though he were talking to a guest:

Welcome, my Sister Death!

(2 Cel 217; 1 Cel 108)

A prayer of St. Francis

With this prayer, Thomas of Celano brings his account of the life of Francis to a close:

Father,
remember your sons who, as you know,
are threatened with grave dangers
and find it very hard
to follow in your footsteps.
Give them the strength to hold out;
purify them so that they may become shining
examples;
give them joy
so that they may bear fruit;
invoke the Spirit of grace
and prayer for them,
so that they may possess the true humility
that you had,
that they may love poverty
as you did,
that they may become worthy of the love
with which you loved
Christ crucified.

(2 Cel 224)

Praise and Thanksgiving

"He who called nothing on earth his own, owned everything in God and God in everything."
(Bonaventure)

How infinitely great it is
to have a Father in heaven!

How indescribably lovely it is
to have a Bridegroom in heaven!

How incredibly good
and cheering it is
to have a Brother
who laid down his life for his sheep
and prayed to his Father
on our account, saying:
In your name keep those
whom you have given me . . .

He alone is good,
he alone most high,
he alone all-powerful,
wonderful, glorious, holy,
worthy of all praise and blessing
for endless ages and ages.

This act of praise is taken from a longer letter addressed by
Francis to "All Christians, religious, clerics and lay men and
women."

Almighty, most high and sovereign God,
holy and righteous Father,
Lord, King of heaven and earth:
we thank you for your own existence
and because, by your holy will,
through your only Son
and through your Holy Spirit,
you have created everything
spiritual and corporeal.
You fashioned us
in your own image and likeness
and placed us in Paradise;
it was however through our own fault
that we fell.
We thank you for having created us
through your Son;
we thank you for having loved us
with your holy love.
As true God and true man
Christ came into the world,
born of blessed Mary ever virgin;
through his cross,
his blood and death,
he has redeemed us
from the captivity of sin.

We thank you because your Son
is to come again in majesty
to judge those who have refused to repent
and acknowledge you;
while to all who have acknowledged you,

worshipped you and served you in penitence,
he will say:
Come, you blessed of my Father,
take possession of the kingdom
prepared for you
from the beginning of the world.
We are not worthy
to mention your name,
but we earnestly beg
that our Lord Jesus Christ,
your beloved Son
in whom you are well pleased,
may with the Holy Spirit the Paraclete,
thank you for all the great things
you have wrought in us through him.
Alleluia.

And we humbly beg our glorious mother,
blessed Mary ever virgin,
blessed Michael,
Gabriel and Raphael,
the Seraphim and Cherubim,
the Principalities and Powers,
all the Angels and Archangels
blessed John the Baptist,
John the Evangelist,
Peter and Paul,
the Patriarchs, Prophets,
Innocents,
Apostles, Evangelists, Disciples,
Martyrs, Confessors, Virgins,

blessed Elias and Enoch
and the other saints, dead,
living or still to come,
that they may give thanks for everything
to you, Father, most high, eternal,
true and living God,
your dearly beloved Son
our Lord Jesus Christ
and the Holy Spirit the Paraclete
forever and ever.

As in the Preface to the Eucharistic Sacrifice, so in this act of
praise, the whole divine plan of creation and redemption is
passed in review. This song of thanksgiving, combining many
written sources, occurs in Chapter 23 of the "unconfirmed"
Rule composed between 1210 and 1221.

Fear God and glorify him!
You are worthy, Lord,
to receive honor and praise.
Praise the Lord, and you who fear him.
Hail, Mary, full of grace,
the Lord is with you.
Bless the Lord, heaven and earth,
bless him, seas and rivers;
children of God, praise the Lord!
This is the day the Lord has made,
let us rejoice and be glad.
You are the King of Israel.
Let everything that breathes praise the Lord!
Praise the Lord, for he is good;
let all who read this praise the Lord!
Bless the Lord, all you his works,
you birds of heaven, praise the Lord!
Bless the Lord, all you children,
young men and maidens,
praise the Lord!
Worthy is the Lamb that was slain to receive
praise, honor and glory.
Blessed be the Holy Trinity
and Undivided Unity.
Holy Michael the Archangel, defend us!

Apparently Francis inscribed these invocations with his own
hand on a wooden tablet. It was intended for the altar of
hermitage at Cesi di Termi in Umbria.

Let us bow down,
let earth adore
and heaven exult
when, by means of the priest,
Christ the Son of the Living God
is present on the altar.

What admirable dignity!
What amazing condescension!
What sublime lowliness!
What lowly sublimity!
That the Lord of all,
the Divine Son of the Father,
should make himself so small!
To rescue us, he hides
under the homely form of bread.

Francis then exhorts the brothers:

Observe God's humility,
offer him your whole heart!
Be humble yourselves,
to be exalted with him!
Keep nothing back for yourselves
so that he who has given himself to you
can make you altogether his.

From the letter addressed by Francis to all the brothers of the
Order in about 1220.

Almighty, eternal,
just and merciful God,
grant us in our misery to do
for your sake alone
what we know you want us to do,
and always to want what pleases you;
so that, cleansed and enlightened within
and inflamed by the fire of the Holy Spirit,
we may be able to follow in the footsteps
of your Son, our Lord Jesus Christ,
and so make our way to you, Most High,
by your grace alone—
you who live and reign
in perfect Trinity
and simple Unity,
and are glorified,
God almighty,
forever and ever.

With this prayer Francis closes his letter "To all the brothers
of the Order" (see previous page).

Our Creator, Redeemer and Savior,
you are the only true God,
in you is the fullness of goodness,
you are the true and sovereign good.
You alone are good,
loving, gentle, sweet and lovable,
holy, just, true and fair,
kind, innocent and pure.
In you is all pardon,
grace and glory
for all the repentant,
for the just,
for all who share your joy in heaven.
Let nothing separate us from you.
Everywhere, at any place,
at any hour and at any time,
daily, ceaselessly,
let us truly and humbly
believe in you,
love, honor and worship,
praise, bless and glorify you,
serve you and give thanks to you,
most high, sovereign, eternal God,
Trinity and Unity,
Father, Son and Holy Spirit,
Creator of all things
and Savior of all who have faith in you,
who put their hope in you
and who love you.
You are without beginning or end,
unchanging, invisible,

ineffable and inscrutable;
you are sublime and great,
mild and lovable,
the source of joy.
We desire you
above all else
forever and ever. Amen.

An act of praise from Chapter 23 of the unconfirmed Rule of
1221, rephrased in the form of a prayer.

Holy, holy, holy is the Lord
God Almighty,
who is, who was and who is to come.

Let us praise and glorify him forever.

You are worthy, Lord our God,
to receive praise and glory,
honor and blessing.

Let us praise and glorify him forever.

Worthy is the Lamb that was slain
to receive divine power,
wisdom and strength,
honor, glory and blessing.

Let us praise and glorify him forever.

Bless the Lord,
all you works of the Lord.

Let us praise and glorify him forever.

Praise our God,
all you his servants,
honor him, you who fear God,
small and great.

Let us praise and glorify him forever.

Let heaven and earth praise your glory:
all creatures in heaven, on earth
and under the earth,
the sea and everything in it.

Let us praise and glorify him forever.

Glory be to the Father and to the Son
and to the Holy Spirit.

Let us praise and glorify him forever.

As it was in the beginning, is now
and ever shall be, world without end. Amen.

Let us praise and glorify him forever.

All-powerful, all holy,
most high and supreme God,
sovereign good,
all good, every good,
you who alone are good:
it is to you we must give
all praise, all glory,
all thanks, all honor, all blessing;
to you we must refer
all good always.

"Francis made a point of repeating these praises as often as possible (for instance, always before saying his Office, see pp. 79ff). And he also taught his brothers to recite these prayers with love and devotion" (*Mirror of Perfection* lxxxii).

Paraphrase of the Lord's Prayer

Our Father most holy,
our Creator and Redeemer,
our Savior and our Comforter.

Who art in heaven
in the angels and the saints,
giving them light to know you,
since you, Lord, are light;
setting them afire to love you,
since you, Lord, are love;
dwelling in them
and giving them fullness of joy,
since you, Lord,
are the supreme, eternal good,
and all good comes from you.

Hallowed be thy name:
may we grow to know you better and better
and so appreciate
the extent of your favors,
the scope of your promises,
the sublimity of your majesty
and the profundity of your judgements.

Thy kingdom come,
so that you may reign in us by your grace
and bring us to your kingdom,
where we shall see you clearly,
love you perfectly
and, happy in your company,
enjoy you forever.

Thy will be done
on earth as it is in heaven,
so that we may love you
with all our heart
by always having you in mind;
with all our soul
by always longing for you;
with all our mind
by determining
to seek your glory in everything;
and with all our strength
of body and soul
by lovingly serving you alone.
May we love our neighbors as ourselves
and encourage them all to love you,
by bearing our share
in the joys and sorrows of others
while giving offence to no one.

Give us this day our daily bread,
your beloved Son,
our Lord Jesus Christ,
so that we may remember and appreciate
how much he loved us

and everything he said and did
and suffered.

And forgive us our trespasses
in your immeasurable mercy
by virtue of the passion of your Son
and through the intercession
of Mary and all your saints

As we forgive those
who trespass against us:
and if we do not forgive perfectly,
Lord, make us forgive perfectly,
so that, for love of you,
we may really forgive our enemies
and fervently pray to you for them,
returning no one evil for evil
but trying to serve you in everyone.

And lead us not into temptation,
be it hidden or obvious,
sudden or persistent.

But deliver us from evil,
past, present or future. Amen.

The Praises of the Virtues

Hail, Queen Wisdom!
The Lord keep you with your sister,
pure, holy Simplicity.
Lady Holy Poverty,
the Lord keep you with your sister,
holy Humility.
Lady Holy Love,
the Lord keep you with your sister,
holy Obedience.
All you holy virtues,
the Lord protect you,
from whom you proceed.
No one on earth can possess any one of you
unless he first dies to self.
Whoever possesses one
without offending against the others
possesses all.
Whoever offends against one
possesses none
and offends against all.
Each and every one of you
banishes vice and sin.
Holy Wisdom

confounds Satan and all his wiles.
Pure, holy Simplicity
confounds all the wisdom of this world.
Holy Poverty
confounds all greed, the great ones
of this world and all that is in this world.
Holy Love
confounds all the temptations
of the flesh and the devil
and all human fears.
Holy Obedience
confounds all selfish desires,
mortifies our lower nature
and makes our body ready
to obey the Spirit and our fellow beings,
making us submissive to men
but even to wild animals
in so far as the Lord permits.

Francis addresses the virtues as individual persons, greeting the "Queens" and "Ladies" who serve Christ the King. The Christian life is an indivisible whole, to which each virtue contributes. Hence Francis can say: "Whoever offends against one, possesses none," since this shatters the internal equilibrium on which everything depends.

Greeting to the Virtues

Hail, all you holy Virtues
who, by the grace
and inspiration of the Holy Spirit,
are poured into the hearts of the faithful
so that, faithless no longer,
they may become faithful to God.

This "Greeting to the Virtues" is often found, in the MSS,
tacked on to the end of the "Greeting to the Blessed Virgin"
(see p. 71). Nothing is known either about its date or the
circumstances of its composition.

Where there is love and wisdom,
there is neither fear nor ignorance.
Where there is patience and humility,
there is neither anger nor annoyance.
Where there is poverty and joy,
there is neither cupidity nor avarice.
Where there is peace and contemplation,
there is neither care nor restlessness.
Where fear of the Lord guards the house,
there no enemy can enter.
Where there is mercy and prudence,
there is neither excess nor harshness.

This short song of praise comes from the *Admonitions* (no.
27), which Francis and his companions delivered to their
hearers, to guide them in the Christian life.

Greeting to the Blessed Virgin

Hail, Lady and Queen,
holy Mary, Mother of God,
Virgin who became the Church,
chosen by the Father in heaven,
consecrated by his beloved Son
and his Spirit, the Comforter:
in you was and remains
the whole fullness of grace
and everything that is good.
Hail, his palace,
hail, his tabernacle,
hail, his dwelling,
hail, his robe,
hail, his handmaid,
hail, his mother!

O holy Mother,
sweet and fair to see,
for us beseech the King,
your dearest Son,
our Lord Jesus Christ,
to death for us delivered:
that in his pitying clemency
and by virtue of his most holy incarnation
and bitter death
he may pardon our sins.

Holy Virgin Mary,
among all the women of the world there is
none like you.
You are the daughter and handmaid of the
most high King
and Father of heaven.
You are the mother
of our most holy Lord Jesus Christ.
You are the bride
of the Holy Spirit.
Pray for us,
with St. Michael the archangel
and all the powers of heaven
and all the saints,
to your most holy and beloved Son,
our Lord and Master.

Office of the Passion

*"It was as though Jesus Christ
walked this earth once more."
(From a contemporary chronicle)*

Francis' book of hours

Fixed times of prayer confer an inner order on the course of the day and the cycle of the Church's year. To assure a recurring rhythm in praising God, Francis composed this book of hours. He took individual verses from Holy Scripture, most particularly from the Psalms, and combined them with words of his own to form a meditation on God's love.

It is reported to us that Francis began each of these hours with the *Our Father,* after which came the acclamations (see pp. 62-63), the antiphon (see p. 72), the prescribed psalm and once again the antiphon. And each hour ended with the *Glory be to the Father* and the concluding prayer: "Let us bless the Lord, the true and living God, to him attributing praise, glory, honor, blessing and all good forever."

In his letter to the Chapter General, Francis explained how the prayers were to be performed: "With devotion before God, in such wise that the brothers will not be concerned about tunefulness of voice but about accord of spirit, in such wise that voice accords with spirit, and the spirit with God . . . And I for my part promise, God giving me grace, faithfully to observe this." And he went on: "Those brothers who refuse to observe this, I do not hold to be my brothers. I will not see them or speak to them again until they have done penance."

As well as the brothers, St. Clare and her sisters also adopted this book of hours and—as it is said—by them it was "continually prayed with similar love."

Daily Office

On the eve (Compline)

I have told you all about my life, O God,
and my tears have moved your heart.

All who hate me whisper together about me
discussing what to do.

They have repaid my kindness with evil
and my friendship with hatred.

In return for my friendship they slandered me;
all I could do was pray.

My holy Father, King of heaven and earth,
do not desert me for I am in trouble
and I have no one to help me.

When I call on you,
my enemies fall back;
now I know that God is with me.

My friends and companions
keep their distance
because of my affliction.

You have deprived me of my friends;

you have made me repulsive to them;
I am imprisoned and I cannot escape.

Holy Father, do not desert me,
my God, hasten to help me.
Come quickly to my help,
Lord God my Savior.

Before dawn (Matins)

Lord God of my salvation,
day and night I cry out to you.

Let my prayer reach your presence,
hear my cry for help.

Come to my side, redeem me,
ransom me on account of my enemies.

It was you who drew me from the womb
and soothed me on my mother's breast.
On you I was cast from my birth.

From my mother's womb
you have been my God.
Do not desert me.

You know the insults, the shame,
the ignominy I endure.

Every one of my oppressors
is known to you.
Insult has broken my heart beyond cure.

I looked for sympathy
but there was none;
for comforters —
not one was to be found.

The arrogant, O God, have risen against me,
a brutal gang is after my life;
in their scheme of things
you have no place.

I belong among those sinking into the pit,
I am like someone who has lost his strength,
abandoned among the dead.

You are my most holy Father,
my King and my God.

Come quickly to my help,
Lord God my Savior.

Early morning (Prime)

Take pity on me, God, take pity on me
for in you I take refuge.

In the shadow of your wings I take refuge
until the crisis is over.

I call to my most high Father,
to God the Most High, my benefactor.

He has sent from heaven and saved me,
he has confounded those who were
harrying me.

He has shown his strong and faithful hand;
he has rescued me from my mighty foe,
from my enemies who were stronger than I.

They prepared a snare for my feet,
they bowed down my spirit.

They dug a pit in front of me
but fell into it themselves.

My heart is ready, God, my heart is ready;
I will sing and chant praise.

Awake, my soul!
Awake, lyre and harp!
I will wake the dawn.

I shall praise you among the peoples, Lord,
I shall chant your praise among the
nations.

For your faithful love towers to heaven
and your constancy to the clouds.

Be exalted above the heavens, God,
your glory over all the earth!

Nine o'clock in the morning (Terce)

Take pity on me, God, as they harry me,
pressing their attacks home all day.

My enemies harry me all day
for many have taken up arms against me.

All my enemies whisper against me,
devising the worst for me.

Those with designs on my life
are plotting together.

When they leave
they say as much;
all who see me jeer at me,
they sneer and wag their heads.

For I am a worm, not a man,
scorned by mankind, the outcast of the
people.

To all my foes
I am now an object of contempt,
and to my neighbors too:
an object of dread to my friends.

Holy Father, do not desert me,
hasten to help me.

Come quickly to my help,
Lord God my Savior.

At noon (Sext)

To the Lord I cry out my plea,
to the Lord I cry out my entreaty.

I pour out my prayer in his presence,
in his presence I unfold my troubles.

However faint my spirit,
you watch over my path.

On the road I have to travel,
they have laid a trap for me.

I look to the right and see—
no one wants to know me.

Now I have no means of escape,
no one cares if I live or die.

Since for you I bear insult,
my face is covered with shame.

I am estranged from my brothers,
alienated from my own mother's sons.

Because, Holy Father,
I am eaten up with zeal for your house,
the insults directed at you fall on me.

Gladly they ganged up together,
these scourges had ganged up together
against me, but I did not realize.

Those who hate me for no reason
now outnumber the hairs on my head.

My enemies wrongfully persecuting me
have grown too strong for me.

Must I give back
what I did not steal?

False witnesses come forward,
asking me questions I cannot answer.

They repay my good with evil,
they slander me
for following a righteous path.

You are my most holy Father,
my King and my God.

Come quickly to my help,
Lord God my Savior.

Three o'clock in the afternoon (None)

All you who pass this way
attend and see if there is any sorrow
like my sorrow.

A pack of dogs surrounds me,
a gang of villains closing in on me.

They stare at me and gloat,
they divide up my garments
and throw lots for my clothes.

They have pierced my hands and feet,
they have counted all my bones.

Like lions ravening and roaring
they open their jaws at me.

Like water, I am trickling away,
my bones are all disjointed.

My heart has turned to wax
melting away inside me.

My strength has dried up like a potsherd,
my tongue sticks to my gums.

They have given me gall to eat
and vinegar to quench my thirst.

You have laid me in the dust of death,
and to my pain
they have added new wounds.

I fell asleep and now I have risen again,
and my Father most holy has welcomed
me into glory.

Holy Father, you have taken me by the hand,
you have led me as you saw fit
and received me into glory.

Who else is there for me in heaven,
and besides you what can I desire on earth?

Be still and acknowledge that I am God,
supreme over nations,
supreme over the world.

Blessed be the Lord God of Israel;
he redeems the lives of his servants
with his most precious blood;
no one incurs guilt who takes refuge in him.

We know that he is coming
to mete out justice on earth.

In the evening (Vespers)

Clap your hands, all you peoples,
acclaim God with shouts of joy.

For the Lord, the Most High,
is to be dreaded,
the Great King of the whole world.

For the Father of heaven,
most holy, our King,
sent his beloved Son from on high,
before all ages,
the author of saving acts on earth.

Let the heavens be glad and earth rejoice,
the sea and all within it resound,
the fields and all within them exult.

Sing the Lord a new song,
sing to the Lord, all you lands.

For great is the Lord
and mightily to be praised,
awesome is he beyond all other gods.

Pay tribute to the Lord,
you families of nations,
tribute of glory and praise to the Lord,
tribute to the Lord of the glory due his name.

Offer him your hearts,
take up his holy cross

and live by his most holy commandments
to the last.

Let the whole earth tremble before him;
Say among the nations: The Lord is King.

*From the Feast of the Ascension until advent,
the following verses are to be added:*

He ascended into heaven
and sits at the right hand
of the most holy Father in heaven.

Be exalted above the heavens, God,
your glory over all the earth!

We know that he is coming
to mete out justice on earth.

In Eastertide

On the eve (Compline)[1]

Be pleased, God, to rescue me,
Lord, come quickly and help me.

Shame and dismay to those
who seek my life!

Back with them! Let them be humiliated
who delight in my misfortunes.

Let them retire in their shame
who say: This serves you right!

But joy and happiness in you
to all who seek you.

Let them ceaselessly cry: God is great!
who love your saving power.

But I am poor and needy,
God, come quickly to me!

Lord, my helper, my Savior,
do not delay!

1. *Ps 69 Vlg.*

On Easter Sunday (Matins)

Sing a new song to the Lord
for he has done wondrous deeds.

His right hand, his holy arm,
has sanctified his Son.

The Lord has made known his saving power,
has manifested his justice
for the nations to see.

By day the Lord bestows his grace,
the night rings with his praises.

This is the day the Lord has made,
let us be glad and rejoice in it.

Blessed is he who comes
in the name of the Lord:
the Lord God has appeared to us.

Let the heavens be glad and earth rejoice,
the sea and all within it resound,
the fields and all within them exult.

Pay tribute to the Lord,
you families of nations,
tribute of glory and praise to the Lord,
tribute to the Lord of the glory due his name.

*On the Feast of the Ascension the following
verses are to be added:*

Sing to God, you kingdoms of the earth,
chant a hymn to the Lord,
chant a hymn to God as he ascends
the highest heaven towards the east.

His voice will ring out mightily:
Give glory to God for Israel!
See his power and might in the clouds!

God is wonderful in his saints.
The God of Israel it is
who gives strength and power to his people.
Blessed be God.

On Sundays and major feastdays

Nine o'clock in the morning (Terce)

Shout joyfully to God, all the earth,
sing praise to his name,
proclaim his glorious praise.

Say to God: How tremendous your deeds are!
On account of your great strength
your enemies woo your favor.

Let the whole earth worship you,
singing praises, singing praises to your name.

Come and listen,
all you who fear God,
while I tell you what great things
he has done for me.

To him I cried aloud,
high praise was on my tongue.

From his holy temple
he heard my voice,
my entreaty reached his ear.

Bless our God, you peoples,

loudly proclaim his praise.

In him shall every race
in the world be blessed;
all nations shall proclaim his glory.

Blessed be the Lord, the God of Israel,
who alone does wondrous deeds.

Blessed forever be his glorious name;
may the whole world be filled with his glory.
Amen. Amen.

At noon (Sext)

The Lord answer you in time of trouble,
the name of the God of Jacob protect you.

May he send you help from the sanctuary,
from Zion may he support you.

May he remember all your sacrifices
and find your burnt offerings acceptable.

May he grant you your heart's desire
and crown all your plans with success.

May we shout for joy at your victory
and pride ourselves in the name of our God.

May the Lord grant all your petitions.
Now I know that the Lord has sent
Jesus Christ his Son, and that he will judge
the world as it deserves.

The Lord is a stronghold for the oppressed,
a stronghold in time of trouble.
Those who acknowledge your name
can rely on you.

Blessed be the Lord my God,
for you have helped me,
you were my stronghold
when I was in trouble.

To you, my defender, will I sing:
My citadel is God himself,
the God who loves me.

Three o'clock in the afternoon (None)

In you, Lord, I take refuge,
let me not be put to shame.
In your righteousness
rescue me, deliver me.

Bow your ear to me
and save me.
Be my protector,
a stronghold to keep me safe.

For you, God, are my hope,
my trust, Lord, from my youth.

On you I have depended from birth,
from my mother's womb
you have been my strength;
constant has been my hope in you.

Let my mouth be full of praise,
for me to sing your glory,
your greatness all day long.

Answer me, Lord,
for your faithful love is generous;
turn to me in the fullness of your mercies.

And do not turn away from your servant;
be quick to answer me,
for I am in trouble.

Blessed be the Lord my God,
for you have helped me,

you were my stronghold
when I was in trouble.

To you, my defender, will I sing:
My citadel is God himself,
the God who loves me.

In Advent

On the eve (Compline)[1]

How long, Lord, will you forget me?
Forever?
How long will you turn your face
away from me?

How long must I harbor sorrow in my soul,
grief in my heart day after day?
How long is my enemy to triumph over me?

Look down and answer me, Lord my God.
Grant my eyes light
or I shall fall into the sleep of death
and my foe will claim: I have overpowered
him!
and my enemies have the pleasure
of seeing me stumble.

But I have put my trust in your mercy.
May my heart rejoice in your saving help.

I shall sing to the Lord
for his generosity to me.

1. *Ps 12 Vlg.*

Before dawn (Matins)

I shall give thanks to you,
Lord, most holy Father,
King of heaven and earth,
for you have comforted me.

You, God, being my Savior,
I shall act with confidence
and without fear.

The Lord is my strength
and my praise,
and he has been my Savior.

Your right hand, Lord,
has mightily shown its power,
your right hand, Lord,
has struck the enemy,
in your abounding glory
you have put down my foes.

Let the poor see this and rejoice:
whoever seeks God will find life.

Let heaven and earth give praise,
the sea and everything that moves in it.

For God will save Zion,
the towns of Judah will be rebuilt.
And they will dwell there,
receiving it by inheritance.

The descendants of his servants

will own it;
those who love his name
will live there.

At Christmas

At each of the canonical hours

Sing for joy to God our strength,
cry jubilee to the Lord,
the true and living God,
with the voice of exultation.

For the Lord, the Most High,
is to be dreaded,
the Great King of the whole world.

Our most holy Father in heaven,
our King before time was,
has sent his beloved Son from on high
to be born of the blessed
and holy Virgin Mary.

He will cry out to me:
You are my Father.
And I shall make him my firstborn,
high above all earthly kings.

By day the Lord bestows his grace,
the night rings with his praises.

This is the day the Lord has made,
let us be glad and rejoice in it.

To us this holiest and dearest son is given,
for our sake a child is born by the wayside
and laid in a manger
because there was no room for him in the inn.

Glory to God in the highest,
and on earth peace
to men of good will.

Let the heavens be glad and earth rejoice,
the sea and all within it resound,
the fields and all within them exult.

Sing the Lord a new song,
sing to the Lord, all you lands.

For great is the Lord
and mightily to be praised,
awesome is he beyond all other gods.

Pay tribute to the Lord,
you families of nations,
tribute of glory and praise to the Lord,
tribute to the Lord of the glory due his name.

Offer him your hearts,
take up his holy cross
and live by his most holy commandments
to the last.

Francis:
a Portrait by Thomas of Celano

A very eloquent man, of cheerful countenance, of kindly aspect, free from cowardice and devoid of arrogance. He was of middle height, inclining to shortness; his head was of moderate size and round; his face somewhat long and prominent, his forehead smooth and small; his eyes were black, of moderate size and with a candid look; his hair was dark, his eyebrows straight, his nose symmetrical, thin and straight, his ears upright but small, his temples smooth. His words were kindly, fiery and penetrating; his voice was powerful, sweet-tones, clear and sonorous. His teeth were set close together, white and even; his lips thin and fine, his beard black and rather scanty, his neck slender; his shoulders straight, his arms short, his hands attenuated, with long fingers and nails; his legs slight, his feet small, his skin fine and his flesh very spare. His clothing was rough, his sleep very brief, his hand most bountiful.

How fair, how bright, how glorious he appeared in innocency of life, in simplicity of word, in purity of heart, in the love of God, in charity to the brothers, in ardent obedience, in willing submission, in angelic aspect! He was charming in his manners, of gentle disposition, easy in his talk, tactful in admonition, most faithful over what was entrusted to him, far-seeing in counsel, effectual in business, gracious in all things; calm in mind, sweet in temper, sober in spirit, uplifted in contemplation, assiduous in prayer and fervent in all things. He was steadfast in purpose, firm in virtue, persevering in grace, and in things consistent. He was swift to pardon and slow to get angry. He was ready of wit and had an excellent memory; he was subtle in discussion, circumspect in choice and simple in all things; stern to himself, tender to others, in all things discreet.

(1 Cel 83)

Chronological Table

1182 (1181)	Birth of St. Francis
1194	Birth of St. Clare of Assisi
1198-1216	Pontificate of Innocent III
1202	Battle of Collestrada, captivity in Perugia
1205	Expedition to Apulia, return to Spoleto
1206	Pilgrimage to Rome
	Hears voice from crucifix at San Damiano
	Disinherits himself before Bishop of Assisi
1207	Repairs the chapels of San Damiano, San Pietro and Santa Maria degli Angeli (otherwise called Portiuncula)
1209	Gospel of the commissioning of the Apostles (Mt 10:7-19) at Portiuncula; earliest companions, Bernard da Quintavalle, Peter Cattani and Giles of Assisi
1210 (1209)	Oral approval of Original Rule in Rome
1212	St. Clare invested with the Franciscan habit
	Missionary journey, shipwreck in Dalmatia
1213-1214	Missionary journey (Morocco), illness in Spain
1215	Lateran Council
1216-1227	Pontificate of Honorius III

1219	Chapter General at Portiuncula (Whitsun) Travels in the Middle East, Francis visits the Sultan
1220	Protomartyrs of the Order in Morocco
1221	Chapter General at Portiuncula (Whitsun) Presentation of the "Unconfirmed" Rule
1223	Approval of the Rule in its final form Francis popularizes the Christmas crib at Greccio
1224	Receives the Stigmata
1226	Death of St. Francis, burial in San Giorgio
1228	Canonized by Gregory IX